'D … Mr Deggas to his friend. … you noticed he takes about ten trips a day on our train? And he takes photos from the carriage window. Not of the seaside, oh no! But of the village and the fields and woods.'

'Why not?' asked Mr Bubbus reasonably.

'I don't know. He seems odd to me. Perhaps he's a spy,' said Mr Deggas.

Also in Beaver by Joan Drake

Mr Bubbus and the Apple-Green Engine

Mr Bubbus and the Railway Rescue

Joan Drake

Illustrated by Val Biro

Beaver Books

For Rhŷs and Nìa

A Beaver Book

Published by Arrow Books Limited
17–21 Conway Street, London W1P 6JD

An imprint of the Hutchinson Publishing Group

London Melbourne Sydney Auckland
Johannesburg and agencies throughout the world

First published by Hodder and Stoughton 1978
Beaver edition 1985

Printed and bound in Great Britain by
Cox & Wyman Limited, Reading

ISBN 0 09 938260 1

CONTENTS

1	The end of the summer	7
2	Exciting news	17
3	Preparations	26
4	The storm	36
5	The rescue	46
6	Forester in danger	57
7	Royal visit	68
8	The end of the story	78

I

The end of the summer

Mr Bubbus had the sad sort of feeling inside that he always felt at this time of the year. It was the end of the summer. The afternoons were warm and golden with sunshine but in the early morning and in the evening, a thick, white mist rolled in from the sea. It wafted about the village before wisping away and disappearing between the trees of the dark woods above.

'Time to close, I think,' sighed Mr Bubbus. He propped a notice-board by his garden gate.

BUBBUS AND DEGGAS RAILWAY COMPANY

END OF SEASON

NO TRAINS AFTER SATURDAY NEXT

'Sad day,' murmured Mr Deggas when he saw it. Mr Deggas and Mr Bubbus were the best of friends and they had their very own railway. They were standing outside the old station which Mr Bubbus had made into his home. It was used for selling tickets and such things. Mr Bubbus had once been the driver of big steam engines and the children loved to hear of those long-ago days. The most eager of the children were those of Mr Deggas and his wife. There were seven: Ambrose, Poppy, Peterkin, the twins Pansy and Posy, the toddler and the baby.

The Bubbus and Deggas Railway Company had two lines. One ran along the edge of the Bay, curving above the sandy beach. The other branched off across the fields and up, up through the woods, past Bathbun Towers Halt and on to the View at the very top of the hill.

The Bubbus and Deggas Railway Company had two engines. Well, one really, Forester, a little apple-green 0–4–0 goods engine which pulled two carriages gaily decorated with birds, butterflies, flowers and balloons, painted by the Deggas children. The other engine was 'Princess' lent to the railway by Sir Benjamin Bathbun, their friend, who lived at Bathbun Towers where he had a wonderful collection of all sorts and kinds of engines which people came from miles around to see.

In the spring and summer, Forester trundled backwards and forwards around the bay, pulling carriages packed with sun-tanned holiday families on their way to go swimming and sailing, picnicking and paddling and building castles in the sand. Mr Bubbus, Mr Deggas and Billy Buttonhook, their newest helper, took turns to drive and be fireman on the engine and everyone was as happy as could be. But now the summer was over. The children had gone back to school and the only passengers travelling seemed to be elderly gentlemen with their newspapers and grey-haired ladies carrying knitting-bags. As Mr Bubbus and Mr Deggas stood there, Billy Buttonhook passed by. 'Oh dear,' he said, 'does that mean you won't want me any more?'

'Of course not, Billy,' answered Mr Bubbus kindly. 'We work on the railway in the winter, you know.'

'I don't want to leave my little home in the signal box,' said Billy.

'Don't worry,' replied Mr Bubbus. 'There's lots to do. Engines to clean thoroughly, carriages to re-paint.'

'What about a little holiday?' suggested Mr Deggas hopefully.

'No time. There is far too much to do,' said Mr Bubbus cheerfully. Billy went on his way and towards the station came a rather large man wearing a bright check suit.

'Do you see this chap?' whispered Mr Deggas to his friend. 'Have you noticed he takes about ten trips a day on our train? And he takes photos from the carriage window. Not of the seaside, oh no! But of the village and the fields and woods.'

'Why not?' asked Mr Bubbus reasonably.

'I don't know. He seems odd to me. Perhaps he's a spy,' said Mr Deggas.

'Not much to spy on round here,' smiled Mr Bubbus.

'He's staying at the village inn. I'm going to do a spot of detective work,' declared Mr Deggas. 'There is something funny going on, I know it.'

Mr Bubbus chuckled. 'Time for the next trip,' he said.

Next day, when Mr Bubbus was tying up his dahlias, Ambrose, the oldest Deggas boy, came whizzing down the lane on his bicycle.

'Come quickly,' he panted. 'Dad says it is an EMERGENCY. Would you like a lift on my bike?'

Mr Bubbus thought not, but hurried up the lane after Ambrose.

'I have bad news,' Mr Deggas greeted him gloomily. 'It seemed that the man, Mr Rondo, was looking round the village for a place to build his factory.'

There were cries of horror.

'A factory . . . how awful!'

'In the village? Oh no!'

'I hear he wants the middle field,' continued Mr Deggas, 'for his GLUE factory.'

There were more cries of dismay.

'Oh, the smell! Our village will be ruined,' wailed Mrs Deggas.

'No one will want to come for holidays then,' groaned Ambrose.

'There won't be anyone to ride on our trains,' added Poppy.

Mr Bubbus went pale. He hadn't thought of that.

'This Mr Rondo must be stopped AT ONCE,' he declared. 'But doesn't that middle field belong to us? When we laid our number two line to the View, I thought all the fields were ours.'

'Aha, of course,' cried Mr Deggas and fetched his IMPORTANT PAPERS. Everyone waited anxiously, but Mr Deggas could not find the right one.

'Keep smiling,' he said, 'if it isn't our field, it must belong to Sir Benjamin for the line goes through his woods and by his house.'

Mr Bubbus, Ambrose, Poppy and Peterkin bundled into the family car and Mr Deggas roared up the hill to Bathbun Towers. Thumper, Sir Benjamin's driver and handyman, let them in and in a few moments Sir Benjamin heard the sad tale. He fetched *his* IMPORTANT PAPERS . . . but he could not find one about the middle field either.

'Excuse me sir,' said Thumper who was listening. 'I'm nearly sure that field belongs to Miss Patty Pettipan who lives in the woods.'

'Thumper is always right,' stated Sir Benjamin.

'Come along everyone,' ordered Mr Deggas, 'to the woods.'

Sir Benjamin joined them and they soon found the cottage. The thatched roof looked as if it needed a good comb, the paint was flaking, and the garden was a tangle of weeds.

Miss Pettipan came to the door, grey hair wisping about. 'Aha, visitors,' she croaked, hairpins falling around her feet.

Mr Deggas carefully explained why they had come.

'Oh yes, the middle field was mine, but I sold it a few days ago,' she cackled. 'To a man with a funny name. Bongo, I think it was.'

'Rondo,' corrected Mr Bubbus. He told her why Mr Rondo wanted the field and Miss Pettipan rattled with indignation.

'How naughty of him,' she snorted, 'I would not have sold the field if I had known that. Buy it back from him.'

'We'll try,' they said and set off at once for the village inn, where they asked to see Mr Rondo.

Mr Rondo came down. He was polite but firm. 'That middle field is mine now,' he stated, 'and I'm going to build a grand factory there. That's that.'

'We'll fight you all the way,' declared Mr Deggas bravely and Ambrose and Poppy felt so proud of their father.

'Oh deary me,' sighed Mr Bubbus for the tenth time as they went home. 'What shall we do now?'

'There are things we can do,' said Mr Deggas who was very clever. 'People can't build factories willy-nilly all over the place. We'll find a way to stop Mr Rondo.'

But next day something happened that set the village in a tizzy and made everyone forget (for the moment) about Mr Rondo and his horrid factory.

2

Exciting news

Mr Bubbus was having his breakfast of buttered toast and a brown boiled egg when the postman plopped the mail through the letter-box. Mr Bubbus did not hurry to pick it up because there was never anything very exciting there. A few bills and uninteresting things like that and now and again, a rather dull letter from his sister.

But today, he noticed a large, creamy envelope lying on the mat. He picked it up, feeling the thick, glossy paper and seeing a gold crest stamped on the back.

'Good gracious, whatever can this be?' he wondered. He slit the envelope open with his knife, making a buttery smear, drew out the letter and read it.

Mr Bubbus turned pale, then pink, then red. 'Well,' he gasped, 'upon my word! Goodness me!'

You can see, he was very much surprised.

Without waiting to finish his egg or even put on one of his hats, he ran up the lane to the house of his friend Mr Deggas.

The children were at school but Mr and Mrs Deggas were there with the toddler and the baby.

'L-l-l-look at th-this,' puffed Mr Bubbus waving the letter about in the air. 'Read it, read it.'

'My dear friend, calm down,' soothed Mr Deggas. He took the letter and read it.

'Bless my soul!' he exclaimed. 'Well, I never!'

'What is it? What is it? What does it say? Tell me,' begged Mrs Deggas, agog with curiosity.

'My dear, it says that *Royalty* wishes to

come and visit the Bubbus and Deggas Railway. Indeed, wants to take a trip on one of our trains,' explained Mr Deggas, with a touch of pride.

'*Royalty*,' breathed Mrs Deggas, quite overcome. 'Do you mean . . . the Queen?'

'Well no,' Mr Deggas shook his head, 'but a royal princess from a foreign land.'

'Princess Cherriplum from Jamfotee,' said Mr Bubbus grandly. 'She loves steam engines, it seems and she has heard of our little railway. She is sending someone to make the arrangements.'

'Fancy that,' smiled Mrs Deggas, 'I saw her picture in the paper once. A pretty little thing, she is. Just think, a princess coming to our village.'

'Riding on *our* train,' added Mr Bubbus proudly.

The news was soon all around the village and everyone wanted to know everything.

'When is she coming?' they asked.

'What shall we do?'

'Where will she go?'

'Wait and see,' advised Mr Bubbus and Mr Deggas, feeling extremely important. 'We will let you know when the arrangements are made.'

Next day, a large, shiny black car with a little flag flying on the bonnet arrived at Station House. A gentleman wearing a bowler hat and carrying an umbrella and a brown-skinned gentleman carrying a brief-case, knocked at the door.

'We have come,' they announced to a rather flustered Mr Bubbus, 'about the royal visit.'

'Come in, come in,' invited Mr Bubbus. He made coffee for his guests and while they were drinking it, he ran for Mr Deggas to come and help him.

'You are so clever at these things. I shall forget half, I know,' he panted.

'Leave it to me,' replied his friend calmly.

Mr Bubbus looked admiringly at his friend as Mr Deggas made notes in a little book, nodding his head and saying wisely . . .

'Quite so.'

'Of course. I'll see to it.'

'Leave it to me' . . . and things like that.

Princess Cherriplum was coming to open a new motor road and when she heard the Bubbus and Deggas Railway was nearby, she insisted on visiting it.

'If she takes a trip to the View,' Mr Deggas pointed out, 'she will be able to see the new road below.'

'I am afraid you will have to open up your railway especially for the Princess,' said the brown gentleman.

'No problem,' said Mr Deggas.

'Splendid, splendid,' murmured the bowler-hatted gentleman. They shook hands and purred off in their magnificent car. Mr Bubbus and Mr Deggas, feeling breathless and pleased all at the same time, looked at each other.

'To work, to work,' cried Mr Deggas briskly. 'First, we must have a village meeting and decide what we are going to do.'

'Oh,' gasped Mr Bubbus remembering. 'We were going to have a meeting about Mr Rondo and his factory.'

'Forget that,' said Mr Deggas airily. 'We can deal with that matter *after* the royal visit.'

'Yes, so we can,' agreed Mr Bubbus merrily. 'Let's just think of the happy things and have a lovely day.'

A notice which had been painted was hastily altered and posted in the shop window of Mr Tims the grocer.

Everyone who passed by read the notice and by seven o'clock on Thursday night the Village Hall was packed to the doors, all seats taken and people standing in every space there was.

Mr Deggas was immediately chosen to be chairman and modestly took his seat on the wobbly little stage. Mr Bubbus, rather red in the face, sat beside him to take notes and the Deggas family sat proudly in the front row and clapped loudly when Mr Deggas stood up to speak. The evening was a great success. Everyone had different ideas about what should be done. As a princess had never been near the village before, no one quite knew what were the PROPER and CORRECT things to do.

But it was decided that the village would be decorated and that the village band would perform. Old Mr Tims, who played the trombone, was delighted at this. There was to be a holiday for the children and after the princess left, there was to be a party tea for all the children on the Village Green – in the Village Hall if wet.

'We must all wish for a fine day,' said Mr Deggas.

After everyone had been given something or other to do, Mr Deggas declared the meeting closed and they all went home, excitedly talking and making plans.

'It's going to be a GREAT DAY,' remarked Mr Deggas to Mr Bubbus as they strolled home together, the children running and skipping in front of them.

'It will be a day the village will never forget,' said Mr Bubbus. 'I can hardly wait for it to come.'

3

Preparations

There wasn't much time before the visit of Princess Cherriplum so everyone became busy at once. In every house, cottage and shop in the village, work was going on.

Old decorations and flags and bunting left over from days gone by, were dragged from cupboards and attics and washed and ironed. In the village school, the children made paper chains in the colours of Jamfotee (red, green and marmalade) and little flags to wave on the day.

In the Village Hall, a long banner was run up from one of Mrs Deggas' old sheets. Painted on it in huge letters was the message:

WELCOME TO PRINCESS CHERRIPLUM.

This was to be hung across the street from Tims' shop to the butcher's. Mr Bubbus gave the doors and window-frames of Station House a fresh coat of sparkling white paint. He cleaned and scrubbed and polished until every room gleamed and shone. Princess Cherriplum would have to walk through his hall on to the platform, but Mr Bubbus wanted his whole house to be just right.

'She may wish to sit down,' he explained. 'Or have a cup of tea or even stay the night, so I must be ready for *anything*.'

He swept the station platform and carefully tended his potted plants, which on the great day, he was to place here and there, to brighten things up.

Then he and Mr Deggas, Ambrose, Poppy, Peterkin, Pansy and Posy set about the two engines, their own Forester and Sir Benjamin's Princess.

'Whatever is going on?' wondered Forester. 'I thought we were having our rest time.'

Princess hissed indignantly as her boilers

were cleaned out. But they listened to the children talking as they were oiled and polished and when they were alone in the shed, they had a little talk.

'Did you hear?' asked Forester. 'A royal princess is coming to ride on our railway.'

'I shall pull the train, of course,' declared Princess smugly.

'I was here first so I think I shall be the one chosen to take the royal train,' said Forester rather crossly.

'Rubbish,' snapped her companion. 'Why, *my* name is Princess, so they are sure to choose *me* to take a real, live Princess.'

'We'll have to wait and see,' replied Forester coldly.

It was arranged that Princess Cherriplum should go round the bay in Forester's train, then change trains to make the trip to the View. After that, she would have tea with Sir Benjamin at Bathbun Towers, board the train at the Halt, go back to the station and leave for home. Mr Bubbus was rather disappointed that the Princess was not taking tea in his little house but in the kitchen of Bathbun Towers, Thumper was up to his eyebrows in flour and sugar and currants and things, making cakes fit for a princess. Sir Benjamin was busy polishing the silver teaspoons and washing his best china teaset.

'Now, have we thought of *everything*?' wondered Mr Deggas the day before the

royal visit as he ticked off this and that in his notebook.

'What about flowers?' asked Mrs Deggas, ironing Poppy's dress.

'What flowers, my dear?' questioned her husband.

'You *must* give the princess a bouquet,' said Mrs Deggas who knew about such things. 'All princesses carry bouquets.'

'I have some lovely roses left in my garden. Will they do?' offered Mr Bubbus eagerly. He ran home and cut the most beautiful roses he could find and Mrs Deggas said she would put them in water overnight, then arrange them in a pretty bunch and tie them with ribbon in the morning. Peterkin was chosen to give the princess the flowers.

'All right,' he agreed, 'but I'm not going to kiss anybody.'

Poppy taught him to bow and Mrs Deggas set out his best blue velvet trousers and little bow-tie to match.

From every kitchen in the village delicious

smells wafted as cakes were baked and jellies made ready for the children's party tea. From every window flags or bunting fluttered and from the school the children's voices floated through the open windows, practising the song Miss Fitt, the head teacher, had written especially for the day.

'Welcome, welcome, welcome Princess
Cherriplum.
Happy is our meeting, happy is our greeting.
We come to wave and cheer you on your
way.
Welcome, welcome, welcome Princess
Cherriplum,
Hear the children sing, good wishes to you
bring,
We hope you have a very happy day.'

From the store-room behind Tims' grocer's shop strange sounds could be heard. Tootles and bangs, squeaks and thumps. It was the village band practising the National Anthem of Jamfotee.

'Oh dear, it *is* a hard tune to play,' grumbled old Mr Tims, blowing the wrong note for the tenth time on his trombone. 'Can't we just play "God Save the Queen"?'

'Certainly not,' snapped Mr Grove the chemist, who was conducting, 'we must honour the princess with her country's tune.'

He tapped his baton on a crate of butter. 'Now, once more. One, two, three.'

The band struck up again, blare, blare, toot, thump and another wrong note from the trombone. In his shop, young Mr Tims shook his head and wondered if the band would ever have it right by the next day.

Mr Deggas was up a ladder fixing the big banner when Mr Rondo left the inn and came towards him.

'Need any help?' he greeted Mr Deggas.

'No thank you,' replied Mr Deggas. 'This is a village affair.'

'Well, I hope soon to be one of the village,'

smiled Mr Rondo undismayed. 'When I build my factory here, I shall often come to visit.'

'Why do you want to put your factory here and spoil our pretty, quiet little village?' asked Mr Deggas angrily, coming down the ladder.

'It's very near to Small Port just around the Point. I can get fish bones and things I need from there,' explained Mr Rondo.

'But there is no one here to work in your factory. There are not many people in the village,' pointed out Mr Deggas.

'I shall bring them in by bus. I'll use the new motor road and fetch in *bus loads* of workers,' said Mr Rondo triumphantly.

'Never,' cried Mr Deggas in ringing tones. 'We won't allow it. We won't have it. We shall fight you every inch of the way. However,' he added, 'you will have to wait until after tomorrow because I have this princess business to attend to first.'

He climbed the ladder again and banged in nails furiously and Mr Rondo went back to the inn.

A few moments later, he shot out of the inn

car park in his big yellow car and roared down the village street, tooting his horn and sending everyone scattering on to the pavements.

It was a very warm evening and people were out and about doing little last minute jobs. The children pranced and danced around and it was all very exciting.

'I think we are ready, I think we have done everything now,' said Mr Deggas with some satisfaction, closing his notebook.'

'Oh, isn't it thrilling?' asked Mr Bubbus smiling at everyone. 'Don't you think it's absolutely thrilling, Ambrose?'

Ambrose laughed then said, 'What about the red carpet? There is always red carpet for royalty to walk on.'

'Oh my goodness, yes. We should have thought of that,' gasped Mr Bubbus in dismay.

'A problem,' said Mr Deggas, 'now, where can we find red carpet at this time of night? Everybody think.'

There was silence as everybody thought.

4

The storm

Poppy was the first to speak.

'I know who has red carpet,' she said eagerly. 'Miss Pettipan.'

'Miss Pettipan?' echoed the others in disbelieving tones.

'Yes,' nodded Poppy, 'she has. I saw it on her stairs when we called at her cottage the other day.'

'Come on then,' urged Mr Deggas, 'perhaps she will lend it to us.'

It was bedtime for the young Deggases so Ambrose and Poppy jumped in the back of the car and Mr Bubbus sat beside Mr Deggas and once more they set off up the hill, through the woods to Ivy Cottage as Miss Pettipan's home was named.

She came to the door looking a little more untidy than last time. 'Aha, visitors again,' she smiled. 'I've no more fields to sell, you know. Did you buy that one back from that Mr Ringo?'

'Er no, not yet,' replied Mr Deggas. 'We have come on a very urgent matter and we wonder if you can help us?'

As they talked, Ambrose and Poppy were trying to peer around the door at the stairs. Miss Pettipan was delighted to lend her red stair carpet.

'Certainly, certainly,' she agreed. 'Roll it up and take it with you.'

They all helped to take the carpet from the stairs. It was thick with dust which rose in clouds as they rolled it up and made them cough and sneeze.

'It's lovely carpet, Miss Pettipan,' Poppy remarked politely between sneezes. 'It isn't a bit worn out.'

'Of course not,' said Miss Pettipan. 'I never walk on it. I never go upstairs. Never.'

'Thank you very much, Miss Pettipan,' panted Mr Bubbus as he and Mr Deggas pushed the fat roll of carpet into the car boot. 'This will be lovely for the Princess to walk on. Are you coming to the village to see her tomorrow?'

'I've seen many *Crowned Heads* in my time,' declared Miss Pettipan. 'I don't think I'll bother to come and see another.'

Ambrose and Poppy giggled together in the back of the car as they drove home.

'I *am* looking forward to seeing that *Crowned Head* tomorrow,' chuckled Ambrose.

'I think Miss Pettipan is a witch,' said Poppy. 'Did you see her cat? She looked a real witch's cat to me.'

'Don't talk nonsense, children,' ordered Mr Deggas, but Mr Bubbus turned around and gave them a big wink.

Mrs Deggas tut-tutted when she saw the dusty carpet but soon whisked her vacuum cleaner over it, making it look like new. Mr Bubbus and Mr Deggas took the carpet down to Station House.

'Now, we *are* ready for tomorrow,' sighed Mr Deggas thankfully. He said goodnight and went home.

Somehow Mr Bubbus could not settle down.

'I'll just give Forester a little run to make sure everything is right,' he thought to himself, so he set off down the line in the autumn dusk.

'My word, it *is* a warm night,' Mr Bubbus said aloud, mopping his brow with his hankie.

Forester was ready coaled and Mr Bubbus soon had the fire roaring and the steam rising. Gently he took her and the two decorated coaches up and down the line, finishing at Station House.

'I think I'll leave the train here overnight,' thought Mr Bubbus. 'It will save time tomorrow.'

Giving his engine a loving pat, he went in his house and as he did so, from afar off there came the distant rumble of thunder.

'Thunder, oh no,' gasped Mr Bubbus, in dismay. There was a flash of lightning so he hurried inside and closed the door. He set about making himself some supper, a few meat sandwiches and some cocoa and all the time the thunder rumbled nearer and nearer. Suddenly a cold wind blew through the house, making doors slam and windows rattle and as Mr Bubbus ran round closing and fastening everything, the rain began to fall, hissing, pelting down in torrents.

'Oh no,' groaned Mr Bubbus thinking of the decorated village. 'Oh no!'

The wind blew, the lightning flashed, the thunder crashed . . . it was a terrible storm.

'Everything will be ruined,' Mr Bubbus nearly wept as he imagined what was happening to the flags and the bunting.

Up in the village, Mr and Mrs Deggas looked helplessly out of their streaming windows. As the lightning flashed, they could see strings of flags torn and whipped by the wind.

'There will be nothing left for tomorrow,' sobbed Mrs Deggas.

'There, there, my dear,' comforted Mr Deggas, 'perhaps it will soon be over.'

Mr Deggas was wrong. The storm raged on, sometimes seeming to roll away into the distance. Then people looked at each other and said, 'Oh good, it's going.'

But with a great flash of lightning and a huge clap of thunder, it was back again.

Ambrose and Poppy were out of bed, peeping through the curtains.

'Oh, why did it have to come tonight?' cried Poppy. 'Why didn't it wait until after the princess had been. Oh, isn't it *awful*?'

'Rotten,' agreed Ambrose with feeling. 'There goes the banner!'

'I'm not looking any more,' wailed Poppy and went back to bed, pulling the blankets over her head.

Mr Bubbus was wondering whether it would be better to go to bed or stay up, and have some more cocoa, when he heard a thudding on his front door.

'Goodness, who can it be in this terrible storm?' he wondered, hurrying to open it.

The door flew open in the wind and there on the step, hair and bright check suit dripping wet, stood Mr Rondo.

'Come in, come in,' invited Mr Bubbus, struggling to close the door. 'What a night!'

'What a night indeed,' agreed Mr Rondo, standing in his wet clothes, a small puddle of water forming round his feet.

'Come over here,' said Mr Bubbus switching on his gas fire. 'Take off those wet things and I'll find you something to wear.'

Mr Bubbus didn't like Mr Rondo very much but he was a kind man and felt he had to help him. Soon Mr Rondo (who was very tall) was looking rather strange in Mr Bubbus' second-best trousers and the white sweater Mr Bubbus (who was rather short) wore when he played cricket for the village eleven. They sat by the fire drinking cocoa and eating custard cream biscuits.

The rain drummed on the roof and the thunder rolled as Mr Rondo explained what had happened.

'Went to town for the evening in the car,' he said. 'On the way back, I found the lane to the village was flooded. There's a hollow up there and the car got stuck in the water. I had to climb out and as your house was nearer than the village, I waded down here.'

'I know that bit of road,' nodded Mr Bubbus. 'It does flood in heavy rain. You are welcome to stay here until the storm is over.'

'Very kind. Thank you,' said Mr Rondo gratefully. 'This is very cosy, I must say.'

At that moment, there was a loud BOOM overhead.

'That wasn't thunder,' gasped Mr Rondo, nearly spilling his cocoa. 'Whatever was it?'

'Hush,' whispered Mr Bubbus. 'Listen.'

5

The rescue

They sat in their chairs, cups halfway to their mouths, listening. BOOM. After a few minutes it came, a sound heard above the noise of the storm.

'There it is again,' cried Mr Rondo in alarm.

'It's rockets,' explained Mr Bubbus, jumping up and scattering crumbs on the rug. 'That means a ship needs help. It's a signal for the lifeboat.'

'Terrible, terrible,' said Mr Rondo, helping himself to another biscuit.

Bang, bang. 'Goodness, someone else at the door,' exclaimed Mr Bubbus, surprised. This time it was Billy Buttonhook, blinking through his spectacles in the light, his sou'-wester and macintosh streaming with rain.

'Billy, come in, come in, whatever are you doing out in this storm?' questioned Mr Bubbus.

'Come for help,' panted Billy. 'Ship in distress, must get help.'

'Now, now, get your breath back and tell us what has happened,' said Mr Bubbus gently.

'I was in my house,' Billy Buttonhook began. 'It was blowing so hard I could feel the old signal box shaking. I was looking out to sea, watching the storm, when I saw this little boat being tossed about the waves. Terrible the waves are tonight, high as a house.'

'Great Scot,' said Mr Rondo.

'Go on, Billy, go on,' urged Mr Bubbus.

'I watched this boat and it was blown nearer and nearer the rocks at the Point,' Billy Buttonhook continued. 'I could see something awful was going to happen. Then they sent up a rocket. I put on my mac and wellies and ran up the line for help.'

'That boat will be wrecked on the rocks before the lifeboat can get there from Small Port,' said Mr Bubbus.

'Can't we help?' asked Billy. 'Could we do anything, Mr Bubbus?'

'I can do something,' offered Mr Rondo. 'I'm a strong sort of chap.'

'We can try,' declared Mr Bubbus. 'I have an idea. It may not work, but we can try.'

'What, what, tell us?' begged Billy Buttonhook and Mr Rondo.

'Forester's fire may not be out yet. Billy, go and get up steam as fast as you can and uncouple the carriages. Hurry,' ordered Mr Bubbus.

'Right,' said Billy Buttonhook, rushing out into the storm.

'Now, Mr Rondo,' went on Mr Bubbus briskly, 'there is an old mac and boots in that cupboard. Put them on, then fetch ropes and cords, anything like that you can find in the shed.'

'Right away,' said Mr Rondo, doing as he was told.

Mr Bubbus found his big torch, then put on his own rain-hat, mac and boots and hastily scribbled a note, which he left on the table.

'Come on,' he commanded Mr Rondo, who was standing loaded with coils of ropes around his shoulders. 'There is not a second to waste.'

They ran out into the driving rain, across the platform to where Forester stood waiting.

'I'm getting steam up,' cried Billy eagerly.

'Let's go then. Full steam ahead,' shouted Mr Bubbus leaping on to the footplate and in a few seconds Forester began to glide down the line clickety click, clackety clack, clickety click, clackety clack.

'Come on, Forester, faster, faster,' urged Mr Bubbus. He blew the whistle three times. Whoooo hoooo. Whoooo hoooo. Whoooo hoooo.

'Why are you doing that?' asked Mr Rondo.

'Mr Deggas knows that means trouble,' said Mr Bubbus. 'When he hears three hoots, he will come to help.'

The train began to round the curve of the

bay and in a vivid flash of lightning, Mr Bubbus saw something that filled him with alarm.

'Oh my goodness, did you see that?' he cried.

'What, what?' chorused Billy and Mr Rondo who were too busy hanging on to the swaying engine to notice anything.

'The sea is almost up to the railway line,' said Mr Bubbus anxiously. 'We must hurry or we may not get back!'

'Oh golly,' moaned Billy, not feeling very brave.

Forester chuffed on in the wind and the rain with the sea pounding at the railway bank and spraying over her. She did not know why she was racing down the line in this terrible storm but somehow she knew it was important for her to hurry. 'Shuff chuff,' she panted. 'Shuff chuff.'

She rounded the bay near to the Point.

'There,' called Mr Bubbus, as the lightning played on the water. They could see a small fishing boat, one moment high in the water, the next almost disappearing beneath the waves, and every second being tossed nearer and nearer the great, jagged rocks of the Point.

'It will be smashed to pieces in a minute,' said Mr Bubbus. 'Come on, Forester, right to the end of the line.'

Gently Forester eased up to the very last inch and stopped with a hiss of steam.

'Now Mr Rondo,' ordered Mr Bubbus. 'Tie the longest rope firmly round my waist and make the other end fast to Forester.'

'What are you going to do?' asked Billy Buttonhook.

'I'm going to climb over the rocks and take this rope with me,' explained Mr Bubbus, winding another rope about his shoulders. 'The sailors should be washed on to the rocks. I just hope I can get there in time to save them.'

'I see. Well, I can do that too,' said Mr Rondo, tying a rope round *his* waist.

'Shall I come?' inquired Billy Buttonhook rather hoping no one would hear him.

'No, Billy,' Mr Bubbus shook his head. 'You might lose your spectacles and then you couldn't see and we'd have to rescue you as well. No. You stay here, keep steam up and make sure our ropes don't come undone from the engine.'

'Ready,' announced Mr Rondo.

'Off we go then,' said Mr Bubbus bravely. 'Keep the lamp alight, Billy, and swing it about every few minutes so we can find our way back.'

'Do be careful,' warned Billy Buttonhook. 'The rocks will be so slippy. Do take care.'

'Forward,' cried Mr Bubbus heroically and vanished into the darkness closely followed by Mr Rondo. Billy Buttonhook leaned from the footplate with the lamp, peering through his spectacles until he could see them no more.

Alone in the storm he waited and watched, every now and again leaning from Forester and swinging the lamp to and fro.

In the rough darkness, Mr Bubbus scrambled across the wet rocks, slipping, falling, staggering on. The waves pounded and crashed on to the rocks, drenching them and swirling around their feet.

'I hope our ropes are long enough,' thought Mr Bubbus to himself. There was a sudden lull in the storm and Mr Bubbus heard something.

'Listen.' He and Mr Rondo stood for a moment panting, getting their breath back.

'Help! Help!' they heard faint voices crying. 'Help! Help!'

'Come on,' Mr Bubbus was off again. Now

they could hear the dreadful sound of the boat grinding on to the rocks and smashing up in the heavy seas.

'Help!' This time the cry was nearer.

Mr Bubbus felt the rope tight around his middle. Glancing back, he saw the lamp flashing from Forester.

'My rope has nearly run out!' Mr Rondo yelled above the storm.

'Mine too,' Mr Bubbus roared back. 'I can't go much farther.'

'Help.'

Mr Bubbus took his big torch from his pocket and shone it downwards. He saw two hands clutching the rock by his feet. He tugged the second rope from his shoulders and lowered the end over the rock edge.

'Over here,' he shouted to Mr Rondo. 'I've found someone.'

6

Forester in danger

In his house in the village, Mr Deggas sat and listened to the storm, wondering if there would be anything left for the princess to see next day. Mrs Deggas had gone to bed at last, Poppy had her head under the sheets and the little children slept through the storm, safely tucked up in their beds and cots. Ambrose was still watching at the window. BOOM. BOOM. Ambrose ran downstairs in his slippers.

'Did you hear that, Dad?' he asked.

'I did. Some poor ship in distress,' said Mr Deggas gravely.

'Oh dear,' sighed Poppy. 'I do hope the lifeboat gets there in time.'

'There will be heavy seas running tonight.

The lifeboat will have a difficult job,' observed her father. 'Now, you two, I think you should be in bed. We have a busy day tomorrow.'

'I'm not tired,' protested Poppy.

'Upstairs,' insisted Mr Deggas sternly.

Ambrose and Poppy turned to go when above the din of the storm, they heard another sound.

Whoooo hoooo. Whoooo hoooo. Whoooo hoooo.

'That's Forester!' exclaimed Ambrose turning back.

'And in trouble,' added Mr Deggas. 'That's our signal. Three whistles means "help".'

'What can Forester be doing out now?' wondered Poppy.

'Something is wrong. We must go and see. Ambrose, put on warm clothes and your mac. Poppy, tell your mother we are going down to the station.'

'Let me come too,' begged Poppy. 'Please, I can help.'

'We don't know what is wrong yet,' pointed out Mr Deggas.

'I can help *whatever* it is,' declared Poppy, with spirit.

'Oh very well,' agreed her father. 'Hurry, both of you. I'll find my big, red lamp.'

Before long the three were hurrying down the lane through the storm. They came to the flooded part and saw Mr Rondo's car there but managed to wade round it and hurried on to Station House.

'How strange, all the lights on and no one here,' remarked Mr Deggas.

'That's Mr Rondo's suit drying near the fire,' said Ambrose. 'I'd know that suit anywhere.'

'Look, here's a note,' cried Poppy waving it in the air.

'"Shipwreck. Gone to the Point on Forester. Make hot drinks. Get blankets. B",' read Mr Deggas. 'Right. Now we know what to do. Poppy, see to the kettle. I'll go upstairs and find blankets. Ambrose, look down the line and see if Forester is on the way back.'

Quickly they set to work. In a few minutes Ambrose was back, his face white and worried.

'What is it, Ambrose?' asked Mr Deggas, alarmed.

'The l-l-line, it's almost w-w-washed away,' stuttered Ambrose. 'The s-s-sea is coming over the rails. Just outside the station, on the bend, the sea is *right over*,' he repeated loudly in case he hadn't been heard the first time.

Poppy gave a little shriek of dismay.

'And Forester is just coming from the Point,' finished Ambrose.

'We must warn them,' decided Mr Deggas. 'Poppy, get the drinks ready. Ambrose and I will go down the line.'

'Do be careful,' warned Poppy fearfully.

Mr Deggas took the big, red lamp and Ambrose his pocket torch. They ran down the line buffeted by the wind and rain and when they came to the bend, there was the

sea, crashing and swirling over the line, washing away the embankment that held up the rails.

'Look,' gasped Ambrose. 'There is a gap now, the water is pouring through.'

Mr Deggas swung his red lamp from side

to side, sea water lapping about his wellingtons.

'Hold on to the fence,' he shouted. 'We don't want you swept away also. I'll try to cross the gap and get farther down the line.'

'Don't fall in, Dad,' called Ambrose nervously.

Mr Bubbus and Mr Rondo, pulling with all their strength, slowly hauled the three shipwrecked fishermen one by one to safety. After a few minutes' rest, Mr Bubbus roped everyone together, then leading the way, with Mr Rondo coming last, they clambered back across the rocks, slipping and sliding, towards the light flashing from Forester. Billy Buttonhook saw them coming.

'Now Forester,' he said briskly. 'Get ready for home.'

'Shuff chuff, shuff chuff,' murmured Forester, steaming nicely.

Billy leaned out, flashing his torch and in a short while was helping Mr Bubbus to untie the ropes from Forester and assisting everyone on to the footplate.

'Well done, Mr Bubbus,' he said admiringly. 'You *are* brave.'

'So he is,' chorused the rescued sailors. 'He saved our lives.'

Although he was soaked to the skin, Mr Bubbus glowed with pride. 'Don't forget Forester,' he said modestly. 'Without the engine and Billy, Mr Rondo and I wouldn't have been in time to save you.'

'Whoooo hoooo,' whooped Forester and reversed down the line with Billy poking his head out to make sure all was clear.

Shuff chuff, shuff chuff, clickety click, clackety clack, down the line they sped, Forester hurrying to get everyone safely home again.

'Here, what's this?' gasped Billy suddenly seeing a flashing red light in the distance. 'Something is wrong. Whoa, Forester, take it easy!'

Hastily he braked and Forester, squeaking,

slowed down and as they came to the bend before the station, Mr Bubbus peered out into the darkness.

'Good heavens, it's Mr Deggas,' he exclaimed. 'What can be the matter?'

Mr Deggas, swinging his red lamp, came alongside Forester.

'The line, it's almost swept away by the sea,' he warned. 'There's a gap under the rails at one place. I don't think Forester can cross it. The sea is right over the embankment.'

'Can *we* cross?' questioned Mr Bubbus.

'I managed to come this way,' said Mr Deggas, 'so if we go one at a time very carefully, we should do it. But Forester won't get over. The rails will give under the weight.'

'I can't leave Forester,' protested Mr Bubbus indignantly.

'I'm afraid we must,' said Mr Deggas gravely.

'Never,' cried Mr Bubbus. 'The sea might sweep her away. If I go, Forester goes.'

Mr Deggas could see it was no use arguing with his friend, so he led the way with his lamp. The three sailors and Mr Rondo followed him, one by one on tiptoe, hardly daring to breathe as they crossed the gap and came safely by Ambrose on the other side.

When they were all across, Mr Bubbus released the brake.

'Now, Forester, it's up to you,' he warned. 'Go as slowly and as carefully as you can or we'll both be in the sea.'

'Shuff chuff, leave it to me, leave it to me,' said Forester. 'Shuff chuff.'

Gently she slid along the lines, click-ety click, click-ety clack. She felt the rails shudder and shake as they crossed the gap.

'Come on, Forester,' whispered Mr Bubbus clinging on and closing his eyes. He could feel his heart thumping and he had a tickly feeling in his tummy. 'Come on, you can do it.'

There was a cheer as Forester reached safety and Mr Bubbus said a little quiet

prayer of thanks. In a few minutes they were all in the warm room at Station House, wet clothes off, wrapped in cosy blankets and sipping the hot drinks Poppy had ready for them.

'We can't thank you enough,' said the shipwrecked fishermen. 'You saved our lives.'

Everyone shook hands with everyone else and there was much talking and laughing.

Suddenly, Poppy called out, 'Hush. Listen.' They were quiet and Poppy said, 'I think the storm is over.'

And it was. The thunder had rolled away at last, the wind died down and the rain stopped.

'What a night it has been,' said Mr Bubbus to Mr Deggas.

'What a day we have to come,' replied Mr Deggas. 'I think we should get some sleep.'

He, Poppy, Ambrose and Mr Rondo went home and Mr Bubbus made Billy Buttonhook and the fishermen comfortable in his spare room and on the sofa and armchairs, then went up to his own little bed and, tired out, was soon fast asleep.

7

Royal visit

The morning dawned bright and clear, the sun shining from a cloudless blue sky. All was hustle and bustle in the village. They were just beginning to tidy up after the storm, when the big tv vans rolled in.

'Come to film the royal visit for the news,' the producer announced to anyone who happened to be listening. But before the lights and cameras could be unloaded he heard about the great rescue of the night before. Quickly he ordered his men to turn around and the vans rolled on down to Station House.

Mr Bubbus, boiling eggs and making toast for his guests, was very surprised by his early morning callers. He and Billy and the three rescued fishermen had to stand in the front garden, blinking in the sunlight, telling their story. How the fishing boat had been driven on to the rocks by the storm and how Forester had raced to the Point, long before the lifeboat could get there.

'We must have pictures of Forester,' insisted the producer.

When they had told about saving the three sailors the producer said, 'Great stuff.'

The camera crew then filmed Forester, who was still by the platform. Poor Forester, covered with sand, festooned with seaweed, with shells and pebbles in awkward places, stained by the salty sea water, her brass dull and tarnished, was a sorry sight.

'Oh dear, oh dear,' murmured Mr Bubbus, seeing his engine for the first time in daylight. 'Oh deary me.'

A police car arrived and after much shaking of hands and patting of backs and people saying, 'Thank you for saving our lives,' 'We can never thank you enough,' and things like that, the rescued men were driven away. The tv vans returned to the village and Mr Bubbus and Billy Buttonhook were left with five hard-boiled eggs and a pile of cold toast.

Hurriedly tidying up, they walked to the village. Mr Deggas greeted them at his gate saying gloomily.

'Look what last night's storm has done.'

There were strings of bunting lying soaking in the road, the big banner was torn to shreds, flags fell limp and wet from poles and windows. Tiles and slates lay smashed in the gutters with branches and twigs snapped from trees.

'Oh my goodness,' sighed Mr Bubbus.

'Well, come along everyone,' said Mr Deggas briskly. 'We have an hour or two before the princess arrives. We must tidy the best we can.'

Out came brooms and brushes and the roads were swept clean. The banner was hastily sewn together (with very big stitches) and hung over the street once more, smudgy but triumphant.

Flags and bunting soon dried out in the sun and fluttered again in the warm breeze.

'Not bad at all,' commented Mr Deggas at last, looking around. 'Just time to smarten ourselves up.'

Six strong men who had been working on

the railway line, filling in the gap with stones and gravel came back saying that the line was now safe and strong again.

'Hooray,' said Mr Bubbus. 'What about Forester? The poor old engine is in an awful state. I can't let the princess see her.'

'Put her in the shed,' suggested Mr Deggas. 'The other engine will have to take Princess Cherriplum on both trips now.'

Billy took Forester down the line to the shed.

'Hard luck,' sympathised Princess gleaming and smart. '*I* am taking the royal train now. You won't even *see* the princess.'

Forester gave a shuddering, sad sigh and worn out with the night's adventures, went to sleep.

The village street was thronged with people, Miss Pettipan (who had decided to see one more Crowned Head after all) amongst them. The smallest children were in the front row at the edge of the pavement, clutching little Union Jacks and flags of Jamfotee. Outside the school, Miss Fitt had the boys and girls lined up, ready to burst into song. There was tremendous excitement everywhere and an air of expectancy as the GREAT MOMENT came nearer and nearer.

At the top of the street, the village band waited, red uniforms cleaned and pressed, instruments shining. Old Mr Tims blew one or two wrong notes on his trombone, just to keep in practice.

Mrs Deggas, Ambrose, Poppy and the children (in their best clothes) were down by Station House. Mr Bubbus, wearing his Station Master's hat for the occasion, unrolled Miss Pettipan's red carpet down the path, through his hall, out of the back door and across the platform to the train.

Billy Buttonhook (wearing a ticket collector's hat borrowed from Mr Bubbus) trundled along the carpet with a carpet-sweeper and a great cheer went up from everyone around.

'Perfect,' said Mr Bubbus, satisfied at last. Station House gleamed and shone, the garden was neat and tidy, the carpet glowing and speckless . . . everything was ready.

Then . . . they heard cheering from afar off and the sound of the band.

'She's coming, she's coming,' shouted the children, jumping up and down.

The little procession wound it's way through the village. First and slowly came two motor-bike policemen, then the band swinging along, ooopah oooopah-ing away

and even old Mr Tims was getting it right.

Next came P.C. Rose proudly marching ahead of a big black, open car . . . and there she was . . . Princess Cherriplum of Jamfotee with her lady-in-waiting and two gentlemen, waving and smiling to the crowds. Through the cheering, flag-fluttering street they moved, stopping by the school. Princess Cherriplum left the car and listened to the children singing especially for her.

'Welcome, welcome, welcome Princess
Cherriplum,
Happy is our meeting, happy is our greeting.
We come to wave and cheer you on your way.
Welcome, welcome, welcome Princess
Cherriplum.
Hear the children sing, good wishes to you
bring,
We hope you have a very happy day.'

'How lovely,' said the Princess. 'Thank you very much.' She smiled at everyone and shook a few hands, then on went the procession, down to the railway.

'How quaint,' said Princess Cherriplum when she saw Station House.

Peterkin (with a little push from Poppy) bowed and gave her the roses, stepping quickly back in case she kissed him.

'How beautiful,' said Princess Cherriplum admiring her bouquet.

She was very small and dainty. Her skin was a creamy coffee colour, her hair long and black and shining. Golden ear-rings dangled from her tiny ears and she wore a coat and dress of stiff rose red silk. Mr Bubbus was enchanted. He thought he had never seen anyone quite so lovely before. Billy Buttonhook had to give him a nudge to remind him it was time to lead the way to the train.

'Follow me, please, your highness,' mumbled Mr Bubbus, flustered, but Mr Deggas, cool as ever, took charge of everything.

'How charming,' said the princess, boarding the first carriage with her friends and Mr Deggas. The Deggas family sat in the other gaily decorated carriage. Billy Buttonhook saw to the firebox. The engine Princess hissed and chuffed, impatient to be away. Mr Bubbus put on his driver's hat and, with a shrill whistle, they were off.

'I'm the driver of a ROYAL TRAIN,' thought Mr Bubbus proudly as they left the station.

8

The end of the story

The 2–6–2 engine Princess pulled the royal train around the bay, turning off by the siding, steaming across the flooded fields and up through the woods.

'How wonderful,' said Princess Cherriplum when she saw the waterfall. At the top of the hill was the tiny platform 'The View'. Here the princess stood and Mr Deggas pointed out the new road far below.

'How interesting,' she said.

The train chuffed downhill one stop to 'Bathbun Towers Halt'. Here waited Sir Benjamin Bathbun, resplendent in tailcoat and top hat.

'How odd,' said the princess to herself.

She had a lovely tea at Bathbun Towers

and declared Thumper's cakes the most delicious she had ever tasted. She admired Sir Benjamin's collection of engines, then returned to the waiting train. Mr Bubbus, too excited to want any tea, was standing by the engine.

Princess Cherriplum went up to him and Mr Bubbus bowed.

'Tell me,' demanded the princess, 'where is your little 0–4–0 goods locomotive Forester, number 1260? I know all about it, you see, but I haven't noticed it anywhere today.'

Mr Bubbus was amazed the princess knew so much about his engines. Hastily he explained what had happened the night before.

'How brave,' said Princess Cherriplum, when she heard of the rescue.

'Forester looks so terrible now,' continued Mr Bubbus. 'I would not want you to see the engine in such a state.'

'I wish to see Forester,' said Princess Cherriplum in a very royal manner.

'At once, your highness,' agreed Mr Bubbus hastily and Princess Cherriplum smiled at him so sweetly that he became thoroughly flustered again. He stumbled on to the footplate and began pushing and pulling all the wrong handles and levers.

Mr Bubbus took the train down the hill, over the fields and stopped just before the points. He helped Princess Cherriplum down and led her to the shed. Flinging open the doors, he announced, 'Forester, your highness.'

The others, left on the train, leaned from the windows, watching.

'How super,' said the princess admiring Forester from all sides. 'I'd like to ride on her. May I?'

'If you don't mind waiting while we get steam up,' replied Mr Bubbus happily.

He called Billy Buttonhook to see to the fire and he and Princess Cherriplum had a delightful chat about railway engines they had known. Before long, from the shed,

glided Forester, with Billy Buttonhook, Mr Bubbus and Princess Cherriplum, waving gracefully, on the footplate.

'Shuff chuff, shuff chuff,' puffed Forester proudly as they rolled past the waiting train where the engine Princess snorted with indignation.

'Who is a royal engine now? Whoooo-hoooo.'

Sir Benjamin and Thumper brought the second train down the line and Princess Cherriplum sat in Mr Bubbus's little sitting-room, waiting for them. Mr Bubbus was so relieved he had given it such a good clean and polish and put fresh flowers on the table.

Princess Cherriplum gave Mr Bubbus and Mr Deggas signed photographs of herself, as she thanked them and said good-bye.

'I've had a lovely day,' she smiled. 'I shall never forget your little railway.'

The procession moved off through the village to more cheering and waving until it was lost to sight.

The end of the story

Mr Bubbus and Mr Deggas stood by Station House gate.

'Well, that's that,' observed Mr Deggas.

'What a day,' sighed Mr Bubbus.

Quick as a wink, tables were brought out and soon the children were sitting around munching potted meat sandwiches, iced buns, jam tarts and jelly with ice-cream. Then, as dusk began to fall and the lights came on, the village band played for dancing.

'Give us something from the Top Ten,' called Ambrose. Old Mr Tims had never even heard of the Top Ten so they played 'Tea for Two' and 'Bye Bye Blackbird' and things like that. Everyone sang and waltzed, did the shake and the quickstep and Mr Bubbus danced a tango with Miss Fitt, all at the same time, and everyone had a wonderful evening.

At last, it came to an end and Mr Bubbus walked home with Billy Buttonhook. They said 'goodnight' at the gate and Billy went on to the signal box.

Mr Bubbus made himself a cup of cocoa. He gazed at the picture of the princess. There she was, smiling at him from the pretty gold frame. There was her name, written especially for him. '*To Mr Bubbus. Cherriplum.*'

Mr Bubbus took out his pen, lifted the picture from the frame and underneath '*To Mr Bubbus. Cherriplum,*' he carefully wrote in his best writing, '*with love. x.*'

Then he put the picture together again and chuckling to himself, went to bed.

Next day seemed very quiet and ordinary. The decorations had to come down and there was more tidying up to do. The children were back in school and life was as usual again.

'But what a day for the village,' exclaimed Mr Deggas for the tenth time. 'What an OCCASION.'

He had come to see Mr Bubbus and they were having a cup of tea together.

'Don't sit there,' warned Mr Bubbus just

as Mr Deggas was about to sit down. 'That is the chair SHE sat in. NO one else is ever going to sit in that chair again.'

'Good gracious,' said Mr Deggas.

'Look,' added Mr Bubbus, 'you can see a little dent in the cushions where she sat.'

'So you can,' agreed Mr Deggas.

'DON'T TOUCH IT,' ordered Mr Bubbus. 'I am leaving it like that for EVER. It isn't every day a princess sits in one of your chairs.'

'That is true,' nodded Mr Deggas, moving to the sofa. 'Hello. I see Princess Cherriplum put "with love" on your photograph. She didn't do that on mine.'

Mr Bubbus went rather pink in the face.

'To tell the truth, *I* did that,' he confessed.

'Bless my soul,' murmured Mr Deggas, surprised.

'I'm just pretending,' explained Mr Bubbus and Mr Deggas said he quite understood.

'Now to business,' he added. 'The royal visit is over. The time has come to tackle

Mr Rondo and his factory.'

'My word, I'd quite forgotten that,' declared Mr Bubbus. 'What shall we say to him? After all, he was very brave and helped me rescue the shipwrecked sailors.'

'I know,' agreed Mr Deggas. 'He does have his good side. But we don't want his horrid old factory here, do we?'

'No,' said Mr Bubbus firmly and they set off for the inn. They were shown up to Mr Rondo's room and there he was, packing his luggage.

'Come to say "goodbye", have you?' he asked in a very jolly manner.

'Are you leaving? What about the factory?' questioned Mr Deggas.

'Oh, I'm not building my factory here now,' said Mr Rondo, hurling his socks into a case. 'Did you see that middle field? Flooded out by the sea. I'm not risking building there, certainly not. Don't want my factory awash with sea water.'

Mr Bubbus was about to say that the sea

had never flooded the middle field before but decided it was wiser not to mention the fact. Mr Deggas was all smiles.

'We'll buy the field back,' he offered eagerly.

'Done,' nodded Mr Rondo.

'Well then, we'll wish you goodbye and good luck,' said Mr Deggas shaking hands, when the business was finished.

'Thank you for your help the other night, you were very brave,' added Mr Bubbus warmly.

Mr Bubbus and Mr Deggas left the inn.

'He wasn't such a bad chap after all,' mused Mr Bubbus.

'We are better off without him and his factory,' said Mr Deggas sternly. 'Look at this village. So lovely and quiet and peaceful.'

'And it smells nice,' smiled Mr Bubbus.

They walked down to Station House.

'How about one last little trip before we put Forester away for the winter?' suggested Mr Bubbus hopefully.

'Why not, why not indeed?' replied Mr Deggas, eyes twinkling.

Very soon, Forester was shuff chuffing around the bay, Mr Deggas acting as fireman and Mr Bubbus driving. The setting autumn sun turned the sky peach and rose and purple and the sea to liquid gold.

'It's a wonderful world,' said Mr Bubbus.

On the following pages you will find some other exciting Beaver Books to look out for in your local bookshop

THE CUCUMBER KING

Christine Nostlinger

It is Easter Sunday morning when the Hogelmann family find the Cucumber King sitting on their kitchen table. Wearing a golden crown, white cotton gloves and red varnish on his toenails, King Kumi-Ori the Two has been evicted from his kingdom by his subjects' *coup d'etat,* and throws himself on the mercy of the Hogelmanns. With his overbearing manner and sly habits he quickly makes himself unpopular – except with Dad, whose reactionary instincts are roused by the royal presence. Meanwhile young Wolfie and his sister Martina make friends with the King's oppressed ex-subjects – and the scene is set for conflict.

Set in Austria, this highly original and very funny story will enthral all who read it.

THE MILL HOUSE CAT

Marjorie-Ann Watts

Gladys didn't expect an answer when she asked the cat his name, but that was just the first of the surprises Oswald had in store for her and the beginning of their adventures together.

THE MILL HOUSE CAT is the enchanting story of a cat with mysterious powers.

EMIL AND HIS CLEVER PIG

Astrid Lindgren

Emil, the naughty little Swedish boy, is up to mischief again! First he paints his sister blue, then he sets fire to the parson's wife, and then he locks his father in the lavatory! And on Tuesday the tenth of August, he does something so bad that his mother won't even write about it in the blue exercise book (but *you* read about it here).

AGATON SAX AND THE CRIMINAL DOUBLES

Nils-Olof Franzén

The small town of Bykoping in Sweden is famous for only one thing – it is the home of Agaton Sax. Being a world-famous master detective makes him a target for the criminal underworld, and two dastardly gangleaders, Octopus Scott and Julius Mosca, fly in to deal with him. But their arrival coincides with that of the unfortunate Charlie MacSnuff and Absalom Nick, who keep being arrested as they are the doubles of Scott and Mosca. The ensuing muddle defeats everyone – or almost everyone!

A wonderful blend of humour and excitement for readers of eight and over.

REBECCA'S WORLD

Terry Nation

Rebecca, mysteriously transported to a distant planet through her father's astral telescope, sets out on an exciting adventure to the Forbidden Lands in search of the last Ghost tree.

This is a rich and often funny fantasy for younger readers by Terry Nation, the creator of the Daleks.

'Undoubtedly the funniest, most imaginative children's book to have appeared in many years.'

London Evening News

AMOUR NOIR

poésie

Aurélien Dony

illustré par Charlotte Sim

À Charlotte

Un merci tout particulier à Laurence Vielle, Antoine Mouton et Lisette Lombé pour leur lecture et leurs retours.

Ce recueil a été spécialement écrit pour la scène et l'interprétation. J'ai eu la chance, dans ce travail, d'être accompagné par les formidables Jérôme Paque et Céline Chappuis (respectivement à la guitare électrique et au violoncelle) sans qui cette aventure aurait été bien différente. Des poèmes ont été enregistrés et sont disponibles en libre écoute sur le site Bandcamp : https://amour-noir.bandcamp.com

« Quand on rencontre quelqu'un de vrai, la surprise est telle qu'on se demande si on n'est pas victime d'un éblouissement. »

E. Cioran

Amour Noir

Tu m'aimes
Dis
Tu m'aimes
Parce que
C'est noir

Dedans autour toujours
C'est noir

J'aime noir moi
C'est ainsi c'est comme ça
Depuis tes yeux
J'aime noir
Depuis nos nuits
J'aime noir
C'est noir
C'est amour noir
Amour noir
Mais noir
C'est
Quoi
Faudrait que je nomme ça dis
J'attends nom pour notre amour
Et moi je dis noir

Peux dire que noir
Peux dire
Autre chose peut-être oui
Peux dire que
Si j'ai peur
– Et j'ai peur –
Je brûle tout
Je brûle tout c'est ainsi
Je devrais me répéter
En boucle me répéter que je n'ai peur de rien
Depuis toi tes yeux ta voix
Depuis ton corps aussi surtout
Plus peur de rien
Mais pas sûr encore de pouvoir dire peur de rien
alors je dis peur
Peur et risque encore
Que je brûle
Que je brûle tout
Tout autour que je brûle
Toi moi le reste tout autour je brûle
C'est un risque mais c'est ainsi

C'est ainsi c'est comme ça
À t'aimer trop j'finis par t'aimer noir
T'aimer trop peur de te perdre t'aimer trop bêtise
et peur
C'est comme ça pas confiance j'imagine en mes
forces et… bref t'as compris

T'entends mon chant du coup comme il est noir
Comme c'est risqué l'amour noir
Comme c'est dangereux
Pas que pour pour toi, amour

Pour moi pour nous
Surtout pour nous en fait
Surtout pour nous
Parce que
Amour noir c'est ruines possibles
C'est destruction là
C'est danger-recule !
C'est peur énorme de te perdre
Alors je brûle
Brûle tout
De ma peur de te perdre un incendie
Un ravage, une ruine
Je redis ruine parce que ruine vraiment
C'est promesse de mort mon amour
T'aimer si fort, t'aimer si fort c'est forcément noir
Le cœur plus du tout habitué à ça
S'était mis à distance de ces mouvements-là, le cœur
De ces élans qui le poussent au-devant des ruines
S'était dit, le cœur, à distance, fais gaffe
S'avait appris des trucs, le cœur, s'était répété des choses avant toi
S'était dit parfois amour mort vaut mieux qu'amour noir
Se contenter parfois des amours petites et des amours quand même
Des amours douces et sans risque, des amours tendres
Et c'est bien aussi ces amours-là c'est pas mourir ces amours-là il disait se répétait le cœur
S'était dit ça le cœur comme un refrain répétait ça le cœur
Amour mou amour mort vaut mieux que l'amour noir

Répétait ça le cœur en boucle comme un refrain
Mais depuis toi
Quoi
Aucun mantra
Pour secourir le cœur
Aucun refrain
Le cœur sait il dit soudain
Il dit répète en boucle
Amour noir promesse de ruines
Amour noir tout brûle fuis dit le cœur
Mais il dit fuis cours pars
Il te le dit le cœur et moi peux pas tricher peux pas faire taire le cœur
Faut l'écouter aussi le cœur
Fuis pars cours
Moi de ma peur de te perdre naît l'incendie la ruine la cage
La cage oui, de cette peur la cage
Dans la cage ton corps, ta voix, ta peau
J'enferme tout, veux tout garder tout près
Deviens jaloux horrible monstre
Deviens bourreau geôlier deviens ivrogne salaud
Deviens tout ce que je crains que je hais
Fuis cours fuis dit le cœur écoute le cœur fuis

Toi tes grands yeux qui me regardent
Fuis cours fuis dis-tu tout bas
Fuis cours fuis
Où courir où fuir où
Où veux-tu que je coure à présent
Dis-tu répètes-tu
Tu dis :
« À ton amour

Noir
Je réponds
Amour noir »
Et tu dis répètes
À ton amour noir
Je réponds amour noir
Que crois-tu que sais-tu
Me dis-tu encore
Que sais-tu de mon goût de la ruine et du feu
De l'incendie des cages et des geôliers
Que sais-tu
Tu dis et c'est vrai que sais-je

Toi tes yeux qui me regardent
Tu dis encore
Tais-toi
Brûle-moi
Brûle-moi plus près
Plus fort
Qu'à mon tour je te brûle
Tu dis tu répètes

Et mon cœur que dit-il
L'abruti ne sait plus
Il bredouille encore
Amour noir c'est
Noir promesse
Ruines
Amour
Noir promesse
Et se tait
Devant tes yeux le cœur se tait

Et de nos deux cœurs muets

C’est ruine ravage et incendie
Nous faisons taire le cœur
Et nous dansons le feu

Se demander

Se demander
Si le geste
Posé
Si le regard qu'on pose
La parole qu'on dit
La veste qu'on passe
Si cela tout cela nous ressemble
Si cela tout cela c'est bien nous

Moi je sais pas
J'ai jamais su
Si les pensées, les paroles et les vestes,
Si le regard, les mots et les gestes
Si tout ça c'est moi je sais pas

Je sais pas
Et moi

Mon je sais pas

C'est pas une fuite un rien
C'est pas le vide tout à fait

Non

Mon je sais pas c'est

Comme

Comme un royaume

Tout petit royaume
Royaume tout petit
Où être vivre
C'est rien

Veux dire

C'est vent
uste vent sur la plaine tu vois

C'est vent oui
a plaine pas nécessaire je m'en passe mais le vent le
vent ça le vent

Toujours météorologique mon royaume
Météo plutôt pluie
Pas triste mais pluie
Pluie et vent
Alors la question d'être, de qui je suis, la question
des mots, des gestes, des pensées, des vestes,
Ces questions se posent pas
Moi mon royaume c'est mort à ces questions de
gestes, de vestes, savoir si tout ça tout cela me
ressemble c'est mort
Moi mon royaume c'est royaume
Où n'être pas tu comprends
Où la question d'exister n'existe pas

Où se demander qui l'on est ne rime à rien puisque
ce royaume c'est pluie et vent et y'a que le corps
pour comprendre ça pour goûter ça
La pluie et le vent
Pas besoin d'être une veste, un mot, un geste pour
la pluie et le vent tu comprends
Alors là au milieu du vent et de la pluie tu vois là au
milieu je suis bien tu vois, je suis bien

Mais mon royaume souvent le quitte
– Mille raisons de quitter son royaume et souvent
on choisit pas faut bien c'est comme ça on quitte –
Je quitte et me demande
Si le regard que je pose
La parole que je dis
La veste que je passe
Si cela tout cela c'est moi
Si cela tout cela c'est bien moi

Je me demande

Et ces questions tu vois
C'est début de frontières
C'est murs et barbelés
Entre mon royaume mon tout petit royaume
Entre mon royaume et moi murs et barbelés
Et soudain plus d'accès
À mon royaume à moi
À mon corps, à ma pluie à mon vent
À mon petit royaume
Plus d'accès

Exilé

Assailli par les questions
Les vestes, les mots, les gestes

Et toi tu viens
Et les questions tu vois
Question de veste, de parole, oui, de parole et de
veste
Et de regard aussi
Les questions c'est couteaux soudain ça me tranche
et m'assaille
Parce que je veux savoir qui je suis devant toi
comment me tenir devant toi veux savoir quoi dire
quoi faire quoi penser
Besoin pour toi d'être quelqu'un
Que tu saches
Si là l'homme avec ses regards, ses paroles et ses
vestes
Si cet homme-là est celui que tu aimes
Tu dois savoir
J'imagine tu veux
Tu veux savoir et je cherche à démêler le vrai du
faux
Savoir quel geste me va le mieux, ou quel geste me
définit, me fait moi, me moule
Alors j'essaie
J'essaie devant toi
Toute ma garde-robe de gestes
D'attitudes
Toute ma panoplie de paroles
Tous les mots pour être beau
Je prends tous les mots pour me faire beau
Bel homme genre assuré
Genre de ceux dont on tombe amoureux

J'imagine tous les gestes, les mots, les vestes
Je les passe les repasse les gestes les vestes les mots
Les passe les repasse dans tous les sens je les passe et repasse t'imagines pas le boulot
De passer repasser tous ces gestes et ces mots

Et toi
Tu viens

Et toi de ta main nue
Défais tous mes gestes

Que fais-tu je demande
Tu te tais
Juste
Tu défais
Tous mes gestes
Tous mes gestes et mes mots
Tous mes gestes
Tous mes mots
Mes gestes, mes vestes, mes mots
Tout sur le sol

Tu dis il pleut
Le vent souffle dehors
Tu dis je t'aime
Et tu m'embrasses

Toi tu me dis là tout bas comme ça tu dis
Viens
Il pleut dehors et le vent s'agite dans les branches
Viens tu dis viens

Tu es beau sous la pluie, dans le vent, tu me dis
Tu es beau, tu me dis, dans le vent sous la pluie tu es beau

Tu dis

Et j'ai jeté mes gestes, mes vestes, mes mots
J'ai jeté dans le vent
Tous mes gestes, mes vestes, mes mots

Tout jeté sous la pluie dans le vent j'ai jeté
Je vais nu de mes gestes, de mes mots, de mes vestes
Je vais nu
Dans la pluie dans le vent

Et toi
Plus évidente qu'un ciel d'été
Toi là
Avec moi dans le vent sous la pluie
Là
Tous les deux
Tous les deux sous la pluie dans le vent

Tous les deux nous noyons les questions
Les vestes, les mots, les gestes
Nous noyons
Tout ce qui pèse en nous

Charpies

Ma peau
C'est ma peau que j'y laisse
Celle hélas
Celle hélas seule que j'ai
Ma peau

Déchirée ma peau
À force de caresses
Et je ne sais pas dire
Pourquoi
Tes caresses me déchirent
Pourquoi tes doigts
– Si doux tes doigts sur ma peau –
Pourquoi si doux
Pourquoi si doux tes doigts
Pourquoi tes doigts me déchirent

Tout
Tout ce qui de toi me vient
– Et tout c'est beaucoup :
C'est regards, caresses, c'est baisers –
Pourquoi
Ce qui me vient de toi
Me déchire

Même regards
Eux si doux
Eux
Même eux
Me déchirent

Qui dit
L'amour c'est miel et douceur
Qui dit ça qui
Écrit ces choses sucrées débiles qui
Qui ne sait pas que chaque geste chaque regard chaque caresse
Déchire putain déchire la peau ma peau seule que j'ai qui

Cachez-le moi celui-là qui écrit amour miel
Quand amour noir feu ravage toujours
Et déchirure

Parce que elle
Bien que douce
Évidente oui
Comme un ciel d'été
Ses regards pas miel douceur ou guimauve
Ça mes couilles non
Elle
Me déchire

Me déchire pour que j'aille loque lambeaux
À travers ville
Pour que tout déchiré je ne paraisse aux yeux des femmes

Que dans mon habit de déchirures taillé par ses regards
Aucune femme ne s'y trompe tout déchiré je suis d'elle je suis tout déchiré
Et c'est ma face lambeaux balafre qui me fait sien
Je suis à elle tout déchiré
Et ma peau seule que j'ai drapeau soudain de notre amour
Et du feu qui nous brûle
Je suis la charpie de nos deux corps qui saignent

Parce que chez nous amour c'est pas repos
Mais feu et sang, cris
Sauvagerie d'enfants pas sages
C'est barbarie et cavalcade
Aux autres l'amour triste des jours gris
L'amour entier, lisse, l'amour gominé des salons,
L'amour maison aux chiens qui dorment
Nous nos chiens hurlent, bavent et grognent,
Mordent et arrachent, nos chiens
Nos chiens, oui,
Les chiens de notre amour
En rage
Pour nous faire l'un à l'autre haillons charpies
Pour être tout marqué
Des chiens de l'autre
Ses mains, ses regards, ses caresses,
Tout ça c'est horde de chiens sur ma peau

Nous sommes à nous deux meute en sang
Et notre amour noir comme une tique
Sur le dos fauve des chiens errants

C'est ça l'amour que l'on se porte
Et nos regards
Même doux
Si doux c'est vrai
Ses regards et les miens
Même regards doux c'est chiens
C'est morsure
Ça nous suit nous taille
Un costume sur mesure
Pour dire en rue notre amour fou
Sous nos regards si doux
Et nos visages d'enfants
Dire qu'en dedans
Nos chiens nous font
Chair pareille et peaux semblables

Traîner discrets
Notre peau déchirée
Et répéter
Que l'amour chien
Vaut bien le prix
De la morsure

Elle danse

Elle danse
La lumière dans l'appartement
Lui fait une piste
Elle danse
Comment son corps
Se déploie plie
S'atomise et se tord
Aucune
Idée
Elle danse
Son œil, sa main, ses doigts
Dansent
Ses jambes, sa nuque, son dos
Dansent
Tout son corps danse
Dans la lumière
D'un jour d'automne
Rue du Pépin 24
En plein Bruxelles
Elle danse

Pour qui pour elle
Pour moi je doute

Qu'est-ce qui
L'appelle
Ou plutôt
La happe
Qu'est-ce qui la prend
Monte d'en-bas
Du ventre

Dis est-ce que ça vient du ventre
Est-ce que c'est naissance danse
Est-ce que c'est vivant
Comment ça nait danse
D'où c'est qu'ça vient ?
Comment tu fais pour être au monde
Sans t'arrêter
Pour que mouvement
Ne pèse rien
Disons soit léger
Légers tes gestes et puis rythmés
Comme moulés
Dans la musique
Moulés dans le son tes gestes
Dans la musique
Et légers tes gestes
Rythmés, légers et continus
Même quand tout
Semble en suspens
Ça bouge encore
Même à l'arrêt
Ça bouge
Ta danse
Même quand tu
Dis c'est fini

Je n'y
Crois pas
Impression que ton corps
Ben continue la danse
Que toi qui vis c'est danse
Comme si musique
Toujours
Dans les oreilles
Comme si musique
Te quittait pas

Pas vu souvent
Des gens comme ça
Première fois vraiment

C'est tant tremblant ta danse
Tant joie sourire et
Pourtant jamais niais
Je veux dire jamais béat
Comme si ta joie
Ta danse
Avaient les pieds dans l'eau
Dans un étang disons
Disons
Un étang sous la pluie
Nourris d'eau
Tes gestes, ta danse
On dirait mouillés
Ruisselante de pluie
Ta joie, ta danse
Est toute mouillée oui
C'est ça
Que j'aime

Ta danse
Toujours un peu
Danse de pluie
Ou sous la pluie
Comme toujours dire
Je tiens je vis je danse
Orages et pluie m'en fous je vis je danse
Pieds dans l'étang je danse
Je danse je vis je danse
Ça tourne ma musique
Dedans toujours
Je danse
M'arrêter pourrais pas tu dis
Et j'entends
Moi si terre
Si lourd
Si pris dans la glaise
Ta danse
Elle me secoue
N'en dirai rien
De plus
De ta danse veux parler
De ta danse veux dire
Rien vu de pareil
Rien vu de mieux
Ta danse à hauteur de toi
Toi fragile menue petite
Ta danse pourtant
C'est tant d'espace pris
Tant déployée tu es
Tant grande tant belle
Tant là dans nos présents
Danse imparable ta danse

Danse à ne plus voir
Que danse
Plus rien autour de ta danse
Tout autour est danse
Les murs, l'espace, le silence
Dansent
Les gens, les tableaux, les meubles
Dansent
Moi si lourd si glaise si lent
Je danse
Et quand cela arrive
Quand tu me dis
Danse avec moi
Moi si lourd si glaise si lent
Je danse
Je danse avec toi
Et suis léger soudain
Suis danse
Tu prolonges ta danse
Jusqu'à moi
Tu me fais danser
Je danse
Avec toi je danse
Moi lourd moi glaise moi peur
Je danse
Tu me danses
Tu me valses
Tu me tango
Tu me colles me bouscules me twistes
Tu me danses
Je danse oui

Je danse

Alors qui
Toi tant musique
Et danse intensément
Qui
Résisterait
Au mouvement de ta danse
Qui
Qui n'aurait pas
Quelque part en dedans
Admis
Sa propre mort ?

Comment fera-t-on ?

Comment fera-t-on
Comment
Nous qui savons
La défaite des autres
Nous qui déjà
Avons tant échoué
Nous qui savons
Les gouffres, les affres
La perte et l'abandon
Nous qui savons
Les corps
Qui vont se déchirant
Nous qui n'avons
Rien su recoudre
Nous maladroits
Dans nos amours d'hier
Nous cimetières
De tant d'instants
Volés
Intensément vivants si fort vivants comment si tant peut-il mourir ?
Nous cercueils
De caresses reçues
De caresses données

Nous mausolées
De corps sueur collés au nôtre
De baisers doux
Arrachés
Au hasard d'être deux
Si tard
Dans un bar
De Bruxelles ou de Mons

Nous déserts de tant de paradis
Cieux pris je crois
Entre Cancale et Saint-Malo
Et toi les tiens
Toi tes images
Espagne à deux
Tous deux collés
Tous deux vibrants
Au présent du voyage

Toi tes images
Toi tes tableaux
Les yeux fermés
Moi mes images
Moi mes tableaux
Les yeux fermés
Nous nos tableaux
Nous nos images
Les yeux fermés c'est sûr
Toutes les images
Tous les tableaux
Les yeux fermés
On les repeint

On les repeint les yeux fermés
Tant nos images et nos tableaux
On les connaît

Tant visité
Le musée des amours mortes
Qu'on les repeint   les yeux fermés
Nos paradis d'hier

C'est dire que nous deux
C'est déserts habités
C'est cimetières ok mais cimetières feux-follets
C'est danse sur tombe nos amours mortes
Parce qu'on a trop vécu
Trop je sais pas mais sûr intensément
C'est que toi comme moi
Jamais à moitié
Les choses, l'amour, la vie
Tout ça qui a vécu, tout ça qui vit encore
Passé, foutu, échec en somme
Et nous derrière à venir l'un vers l'autre
Et se promettre et se jurer
Et dire je t'aime après tout ça

Comment fera-t-on
Hein comment
Nous qui savons

Nous qui savons

Mais savoir quoi ?
Défaites ruines cendres ?
Nous deux si feu

Parler défaite
Et parler cendre
Parler cimetière
Désert
Parler mort
Parler échec, foutu brisé
Dire amour mort ?

Quelle connerie

Répétons-nous
Autant que langue et bouche et souffle et corps
Autant qu'ils peuvent répétons-nous
Mon amour
Qui es-tu
Répétons-nous
Mon amour va
J'ai à te suivre
Au-devant de nous-mêmes

Nuit blanche

Nuit blanche
Écrire cuisine
Sur nuit blanche
Cuisine aux néons
En Wallonie Hainaut

Nuit blanche
Où écrire
Amour Noir

Voilà le début du poème
Je remonte
D'aujourd'hui
À hier
Je remonte jusqu'à la table
Au café
Sur la table
À la nuit
À l'encre
Des nuits
L'encre des nuits
Pour ne plus écrire
Qu'en décharges électriques
En balance entre

Fatigue extrême
Et intense sentiment de vivre

Nuit blanche
C'est lutte
Et combustion
Nuit blanche
Pour Amour Noir
Je ne pouvais rêver mieux

Le hiéroglyphe aux pyramides
Le latin dans le marbre
Les amours aux écorces
Mais nous
Nuit blanche
Pour Amour Noir

L'écriture
De nos déflagrations
Sur la page
Exige au poignet, aux doigts,
Exige tension
Frénésie proche
De l'écriture automatique
Écriture
Accompagnée
Par la lecture
À voix haute
De ce que la main écrit
Au moment
Où elle
L'écrit
Ainsi je lis ce que j'écris

Et à mesure que se déploie le poème
J'entends son chant, sa voix
En même temps qu'il s'écrit, s'imprime
S'arrime à la page

Cette méthode seule
Peut servir
La transmission
De notre amour
Noir
Seule pour être sûr de ne pas tricher
Pour balancer
En temps réel
Le rythme, la cadence
D'ailleurs peut-être
Devrais-je enre
Gistrer tout ça
Là
Maintenant
Que je puisse partager avec vous
Ce moment délicat fragile
Que l'écriture
Du poème
L'écriture sur la page
Ne rendra
Jamais

Amour noir
C'est la voix du poème
La voix qui dit
Dit et répète
Notre assurance
D'être à jamais

Liés
Par nuits, néons
Cuisine
Et Wallonie Hainaut

Bruxelles-Namur SNCB

Bruxelles-Namur
Brouillard
Sur Bruxelles-Luxembourg

Un gars au coin de la rue
Hasarde ses dix doigts
Sur un mélodica

Je passe

Toi
Ce matin
Tu t'es levée

J'y pense
Juste avant
De sauter dans le train

Tu t'es levée

Pas de café
Pas de croissant
Rien sur la table

Que le désordre de la veille

Mais toi debout
Au milieu du désordre
Les yeux mi-clos pour m'embrasser

Bruxelles-Namur
Encore une fois
Et les gens dorment dans le train

Je passe

Pourquoi écrire
Que je te veux
N'importe où mais plus près

Radio Bruxelles

Je t'aime
Allais-je écrire
Comme si cela
S'écrivait décemment
Sur une page
Dans un poème

Je ne peux pas
Charger la page
De ce poids-là
De ces mots-là
Car
Ces mots-là
Ne peuvent s'écrire
Et conserver
Dans l'écriture
Leur sens   et leur lumière

Pas d'intermédiaire
Pour ces mots-là
Pas de page, pas de poème
Pour porter ces mots-là
Alors
Ne rien écrire

Et garder ces mots-là
Pour le moment
Où nous serons deux
À l'abri des lecteurs
Mon amour

En attendant
Je tiens chronique
Sur Amour Noir

J'établis mes quartiers
Dans une salle de classe
Désertée par les mômes

Radio Bruxelles
À Molenbeek
Classe au sous-sol
Où, paraît-il,
Doit se donner
Cours de morale
Un cours dont je
Serais dit-on
Le professeur

Rien n'est moins sûr

Moi je déclare
Je tiens chronique
Sur Amour Noir
Pour toi, pour nous,
Et pour tous ceux
Qui lisent, entendent,
Cherchent réponse

Dans l'obscurité
Aimantée
Des jours mornes
Où les clous
De toutes nos amours mortes
Se collent les uns aux autres
Pour ériger
Palais d'épines
Ceux, celles,
Tristes d'avoir
Trop entendu
Amour toujours
Foutu d'avance
Profite ça dure
Jamais longtemps
L'amour ça meurt
À peine éclos
Tu connais ça
Toutes ces conneries
De cœurs cadavres

Quelle drôle d'époque

Pourquoi s'aimer
Pourquoi forcer
À deux
Les portes qu'à soi
Nous avions condamnées
De quel mythe
Sommes-nous dupes
S'en allant répéter
Toujours Jamais
À y croire aujourd'hui

Plus qu'à n'importe quelle heure
Tout en se protégeant
Du feu, des flammes,
Du risque à prendre
Pour vivre à deux

Quelle drôle d'époque
Pour toi frangine que tes amours
Ont tant déçue
Pour toi frangin
Que tes amours
Ont tant blessé
Quelle drôle d'époque
Pour dire je t'aime

Solitude Radio Bruxelles
Mon amour
Je tiens chronique
Sur Amour Noir
Onde 24
Rue de la Prospérité
Molenbeek-Saint-Jean
Dans une classe
Désertée par les mômes

Et sur les ondes
Répète en boucle
Mes mots naïfs
Mes mots d'amour
Mes lettres à toi
Et mes je t'aime
Jamais écrits

Moi sur les ondes
Tiens à ce que
Soit entendue
Ma complainte pour ceux qui s'aiment
Ont décidé
D'ici tenir
D'ici contourner les prophètes
Prophétisant charognes
À ceux qui s'aiment

Moi dis
Sur Amour Noir
Deux s'aiment
Et s'aimeront
Et tant pis ceux
Pour rire encore
Nommer guimauve
Et sucre d'orge
Ce que je pro-
clame incendie
Qu'ils rient m'en fiche
Je tiens chronique
Sur Amour Noir
Pour ceux qui s'aiment

C'est pas grand-chose
C'est pas bien fait
Ça n'engage à rien ma chronique
Sur Amour Noir
Radio Bruxelles
C'est pas minable
Tout à fait
Mais c'est pas loin

D'être risible
Tant pis je tiens
Et je répète
Amour en feu
Pour esprits vifs
Et sexes fous

Dans une heure
Reprends la route vers chez nous
Et sûr que nous ferons l'amour
Histoire d'avoir
De quoi reprendre
Ma chronique
Sur Amour Noir
Radio Bruxelles

Une rumeur qui nous poursuit

J'entends dans le couloir des morts
Une rumeur qui nous poursuit
S'attache à nous, nous course et puis
Cherche à engluer nos routes

C'est beau comme ils s'aiment, ils fuient
S'aimer comme eux c'est beau, c'est fuir
C'est fuir toujours tout le temps tout le monde
C'est beau peut-être mais
C'est
N'être qu'à soi
À deux
C'est
C'est être seuls dans son délire

Telle la rumeur qui nous poursuit
C'est beau comme ils s'aiment ils fuient

Regardez ça putain c'est beau
Et ça le dit sachant surtout
Que deux qui courent c'est pour tomber
Que deux qui s'barrent c'est pour crever
Que deux ça existe un moment
Et qu'un moment c'est pas beaucoup

Ça se dissipe, ça devient flou
C'est peu de chose dans la caboche
Un souvenir ni beau ni moche
Tout figé dans son sang
Qu'à deux c'est rien on passe le temps
Avant que ne revienne en plein
La cavalcade des chiens-chevaux
Hurlant le bonheur d'être seul

Putain voyez comment qu'i s'aiment
L'un pour l'autre la terre au bateau
Ils disent et rient et sous sourire
La certitude qu'on va bientôt
Se déchirer et se haïr
Que ton pull tiens je te le brûle
Que ton collier vas-y j'le noie
Dans l'eau du fleuve si profond
Ton parfum tourne à la charogne
Tes sourires écailles de poisson
Et tes mains parking où parquer
Les rats à jaillir de nos plaies
Leurs mots tournent, tournent
Tournent au manège
Des métaphores du pire
Du caverneux et du cryptique
Tout suinte l'humide des caveaux
Faut les entendre ces tristes cons
Dégueuler leur malheur
Jeter leurs anathèmes
À la face de ceux
Qui courent à travers plaines
Sans espoir et sans dieux
Sans oriflammes ou porte-voix

C'est beau comme ils s'aiment, ils fuient
Parce qu'en plus faudrait rester
Pas d'ailleurs ou d'autre part
Pas de possible c'est évident
Y'a qu'aux amants
Qu'on pardonne d'y croire
Parce que c'est con les amants
C'est ça qu'i pensent

C'est beau comme ils s'aiment mais si
Soudainement gonflés par un vent du dedans
Les amants lèvent au ciel des bras-chamans
Pour dégager les nuages noirs
De l'horizon de leur amour
Les crétins prophétiques
Les contempteurs de joie
Conglomérats de garde-fous
S'agglutinent et s'attroupent
De tout leur corps font un barrage
Et parlent de la voix
De la raison, de la morale, de l'ordre et la sécurité
Baissez les armes, baissez
C'est qu'on ne vit pas comme on veut
Qu'on ne brûle pas les villes
Qu'on n'incendie pas les maisons
Où reposent tant d'amours déçues
Déçues peut-être amours quand même
Répètent-ils de leur voix morne
Voix de caveau encore une fois
Baissez les armes baissez
Ils sont millions à se lever
Millions de mains sur nos épaules
Millions de têtes balancées

Au rythme fou des automates

Qu'oppose-t-on aux amants-feu
Sinon le job et l'horaire fixe
Sinon le monde dans son jus
Poisseux de réglementations
De Forem en Actiris
De salles de classe en réunions
Pédagogiques ou Brain-Storming
De soirées cool au carré d'or
Des artistes en vogue à Paris
Je dis Paris mais sûr ici
En plein Bruxelles même chaos
Mêmes sourires de pétasses
Et d'enfoirés léchant des culs
Pour un rôle de figurant
Théâtre du Parc à plein temps
Bordel c'est beau nos lignes de mire

Baissez les armes baissez
Combien sont-ils ils sont légions
C'est terrifiant autant de cons
En lieu et place d'espaces ouverts
Et toute la haine qu'ils font pousser
Aux terrains vagues du silence
Baissez les armes baissez
Répètent-ils baissez
Baissez les armes baissez

C'est beau comme on s'aime, on vit
À corps perdus, à feu, à cris
Nous sommes à deux la loi nouvelle
D'un monde où nous régnons enfin

À qui voudriez-vous
Que nous rendions des comptes ?
Rien n'est ici
Vendu à l'immobile
Nos investissements
Dans le réel, ici, maintenant,
Et tout à nous, le monde on prend
Et vos logiques on vous les laisse
Calculs pour cerveaux détraqués
Baissez les armes, baissez
Répétez ça le temps qu'on ait
Forgé la langue des baisers
À même l'humus
Et la poussière
Langue nouvelle et corps nouveaux
Pour se défaire de vos mains moites
Et disparaître
De vos circuits

Regardez comme on s'aime on dit
Mort aux morts et vive la vie

Amsterdam

C'est vrai
Je n'comprends plus rien
Plus
Plus rien
Dans ma tête c'était clair
Il fallait l'écrire – très clair
Je t'aime viens on part
C'était ça c'était clair
Je t'aime viens on part
Et depuis t'aimer c'est partir
Traverser des nuits, des villes
Et puis sentir ton corps, mon corps
Traverser la fatigue,
Transpercer l'habitude
Prendre des trains

Maintenant
Rien plus rien
Prendre des drogues
Chemin vers toi

Les dragons dansent
– Nous aimons les lézards –
Dans nos huttes les hérons

Ont culbuté les fleuves
Et la mer en attend
De grands bouleversements

Tu me diras
Tout ça c'est rêve
Ou poème
Je te dis
Toi
T'as rien compris

Amsterdam, copain,
Amsterdam, frangine,
Qui nous accroche,
Nous appelle,
Ses bras-vélos qui nous saisissent
Et sa nuit d'automne dans la gueule
Ses putes moi je regarde
Et toi tu te marres
J'ai quinze ans environ
Je regarde
Suis gêné
Ça m'attire
Tu te marres

Tu ris même

Je pense à ton corps
Ton corps
Ton corps pays

Un jour exilé de ton corps
Et je ne sais

Plus qui je suis

Le cœur en dedans
Lui si neige si
Si tu sais
Tendre en fait
Ne résiste pas, ne tient pas, fond
Fond à l'idée de ton corps, à l'image
Que je me fais de ton corps
Dans ma tête
Mon cœur fond lui si neige si
Si tendre en fait il fond

Amsterdam disais-je
Lampadaires
Premier joint
C'est tranquille
Agréable
Plusieurs fois je répète
Agréable
Tu te marres
Tu ris même
Et que t'es belle
La fumée tout autour
C'est un film
Cette vie est un film

Et moi
Mauvais acteur
Je m'y suis vu tenir
Un rôle de premier ordre

J'attends le directeur d'acteurs

Le metteur en scène
Non
Le directeur
Directeur de casting

Qu'il me dise

Mec
Qu'est-ce que tu fous là
Dégage
Crétin
Dégage
Remballez-moi ce pecno
Remballez-le

Et se ramène un autre
Et l'autre
À le voir
Je comprends

Le film doit être bon
Je crois que je l'aimerai
Même si je n'y joue pas
Pas besoin d'y jouer
Je veux juste être là, assister, voir
Être sûr d'avoir ma place
Au cinoch des belles gueules

Pour te regarder toi
Fumer à Amsterdam
Un joint tout à côté
D'un type beau comme une pioche
Et qui t'aimera

À s'en fracasser l'être
Tout ça me vient
Sous le lampadaire
Dans la fumée du joint
Tout à côté de toi

Puis merde l'hôtel baby
Retour
En taxi
Parce que le métro
C'est con
Mais c'est raté
On l'a loupé
Alors taxi

Tes yeux
Putain taxi tes yeux
Même maintenant
J'écris
Et tes yeux
Je vais en crever c'est sûr
Tes yeux c'est
Taxi 3h du mat
Et 53 euros
Déviation mon cul
Il nous a bien niqués
On paie on sort et pas d'histoire
On fume
Amsterdam
On rentre à l'hôtel

Bouteille de vin
Dans un distributeur

Dans le hall de l'hôtel

Prendre tes reins
Te faire l'amour

Mourir

Te serrer contre moi

Et Amsterdam
Disparaît dans les draps
D'un hôtel sans histoire

C'est con l'amour

C'est con l'amour y'a rien d'plus con
Tu pars tu quittes tu laisses
L'autre
Et l'autre te suit te prend te cherche

Tu te dis bon
Je sors
J'vais travailler
Faut plus que je pense
À ses yeux, ses mains, ses seins,
Faut plus tu t'dis
Tu sors
Tu pars tu quittes tu laisses
Et boum
L'autre te suit te prend te cherche

Et finalement
C'est pas plus mal
C'est ça qu't'attendais quelque part
T'es tout heureux
Que

Malgré la distance
Et les occupations

L'autre
Te suit te prend te cherche
T'abandonne pas
Jamais
L'autre toujours avec toi
Te regarde et te parle
Te suit vraiment pas à pas
Et toi
Plus possible
De travailler te concentrer
Un truc de dingue
Comme
L'autre
Comme il te suit te prend te cherche
L'autre
Il te lâche plus faut
Que je m'habitue faut pas que je traîne comme ça
Des pieds des yeux des mains
Faut pas qu'je traîne quand t'es pas là

C'est con l'amour y'a rien d'plus con
C'est là ça te prend et rien vu venir
Tu pouvais pas prévoir ça qu'l'autre
Il te suivrait et te collerait et qu'tu pourrais
Plus t'en défaire
Et même que tu
En serais content
L'amour ça t'prend et puis ça t'met
Les genoux à terre
Ça t'cogne et t'prend
Ça t'cogne en plein dans la figure

Alors tu vois

Je me remets à écrire
Des vers adolescents et puis cherche chemin pour transcender tout ça
Par l'écriture transcender, sublimer
Notre histoire, nos moments,
Consigner tout dans mes poèmes
Mais l'écriture en-dessous
Vraiment bas et loin
En dessous de tout ça vraiment
Et si l'écriture parfois touche, atteint
C'est d'la littérature, c'est du vent
C'est pas comme nous c'qu'on vit c'qu'on sent là quand on se prend s'éprend s'étreint
L'écriture elle peut rien

Pourtant c'est con l'amour
Y'a rien d'plus con

Ça te reprend comme ça soudain
T'avais cru bon d'plus en parler
Et c'est pas
Qu'c'était plus possible
Genre grande blessure pas refermée
Mais t'avais admis quelque part
Entre le cœur et la raison
Que l'amour fou c'est bon une fois
Quand t'es gamin
Puis qu'on grandit, on travaille, puis
Faut dire que
S'aimer tous les jours
C'est pas possible en vérité
Et pas la faute de sa moitié
Faut l'écrire ça aussi

Pas tant question de partenaire
Mais juste on se s'ra résignés
Que'qu'part
Entre le cœur
Et la raison

Avec le temps
Comme dirait l'autre
Va tout s'en va et nous avec
C'est ça que tu
T'es dit souvent
Et tu repassais les chansons
Genre les Souchon et cie
Passez notre amour
À la machine
Faites-le bouillir
Mais toi
Les couleurs d'origine
T'en souviens plus
Et t'auras tout
Laissé tomber

C'est con l'amour
Y'a rien d'plus con

Et pourtant moi je veux l'écrire
Puis l'partager à l'occasion
Pas oublier qu'l'amour c'est feu
Et que si tu l'as éteint braise
C'est pas qu't'as grandi abruti
Mais que tu te s'ras endormi
Que'qu'part
Entre le cœur et la raison

Et ça, vraiment, chacun sa vie
Suis pas là pour faire le malin
J'dis juste que moi j'en pouvais plus
Du sommeil du cœur et du feu

Et si c'est con l'amour
Qu'y'a rien d'plus con

Disons que nous n'en parlerons plus

Décision prise
Et sur laquelle
Évidemment
Je suis revenu

Avril 2021

Les demains se déchirent

Nous avons pris mille ans
Nous avons mal au dos
Nous allons presque aveugles
Nos corps ne répondent plus
Ils ont pris la poussière
Nous gardons le silence
Tu dors tout habillée
De peur de le manquer
Le train de l'habitude
Nous passons notre temps
À pister notre amour
D'un bout à l'autre
De notre appartement
Nous nous offrons des fleurs
Le matin des départs
Nous laissons aux miroirs
Des mots d'amour les soirs
Où nous quittons le nid
Pour plusieurs jours
Pour plusieurs nuits
Histoire d'y lire
Autre chose que nos gueules

Qui se cernent et se creusent

Le mal qui nous ronge
N'a pas pour nom usure
Nous faisons face ensemble
À un désastre encore
À déchiffrer

Mon amour
Le vent a tourné
Le vent le vent où souffler dit le vent
Tourne en rond le vent
Entre les quatre murs
De notre appartement
Où souffler dit le vent où
Va le vent va
Lui donner du courage
Le pousser vers l'élan
Le conduire à la porte
Le pousser par la fenêtre
Va vent va
Le vent ne va ni ne tourne
Sinon entre les quatre murs
                    de notre appartement
Mon amour
Ce n'est pas notre échec
Ce n'est pas notre faute

Quelque chose se joue dans ce siècle
                    qui défait nos mains jointes
Quelque chose se joue au-dehors qui
                    cloue nos courses folles
Au poteau de l'ennui

Quelque chose et je crois que les temps qui
s'avancent
Pourraient sonner le glas
Des amours-incendies

Nous leur avons fait peur
Avec nos mots de feu
d'orage
d'averse
Nous leur avons fait peur
toi ta danse
moi mes mots
nos soulèvements barbares
Nous leur avons fait peur ils ont lâché les chiens
les chevaux
les dragons
Le vieux monde s'ébroue
Secoue ses escouades
Des légions d'astres morts
Ont transpercé nos cieux
Se glissent et se faufilent
Au registre des flammes
Ils ont lâché les chiens
les chevaux
les chimères
Tout ça nous mord au cou
Tout ça nous prend aux tripes
Comment s'aimer amour
Comment s'aimer bordel
Des trains pour où
Le vent lui-même
Où va le vent où
Il a perdu le nord le vent et le voilà

qui pisse de peur contre les murs
Noir ce soir notre amour noir
Noir presque cendres
Notre amour-incendie
Noir presque nuit
Noir presque éteint
Noir mais la braise mon amour
Noir mais la braise
Souviens-t'en

Ce n'est pas notre faute
Ce n'est pas notre échec

Quelque chose dans le siècle
périclite et pourrit
Nous n'avions pas prévu de vivre un monde à flics
Ni vivre un monde à masques
Ni vivre un monde à sac

Nous n'avions pas prévu de nous taire tous deux
Nous n'avions pas prévu nos mots dans les tiroirs
Nous n'avions pas prévu les spectacles à la porte
Nous n'avions pas prévu les chevaux les matraques
Nous n'avions pas prévu les mensonges et les coups
Nous n'avions pas prévu le mépris et les claques
Pas prévu le temps plein ni le CPAS
Pas prévu les refus, les auditions manquées
Pas prévu grappiller les miettes dessous les tables
Pas prévu les horaires, les plannings et les zooms
Pas prévu de trinquer aux apéros du pire
Pas prévu les écrans entre tous entre toutes
Pas prévu tout cela, tout ce qui continue
Chaque jour sous les draps de ces banalités

Pas prévu ni Adil, ni Medhi, ni Mawda
Pas prévu Georges Floyd et encore moins Adam
Abattu le jour de mes vingt-huit printemps
Pas prévu, non, nous n'avions pas prévu
Nous n'avions pas prévu et nous n'étions pas
prêt·e·s

Mon amour, tout cela
C'est le monde
Nous nous aimons c'est vrai
Sous ce ciel enfumé
Nous nous aimons c'est vrai
Sous la ruine et la cendre

Nous nous aimons
Et puis
Tu sais
Entre les quatre murs
De notre appartement
Pas dit que le vent
Un jour ne se fasse brise
Et souffle sur les braises
De notre amour à nous
Notre amour-incendie
Notre Amour
Noir

Sinon
Pourquoi vivre
Encore

© Charlotte Simon

© Barbara Maud

Aurélien Dony est né en 1993, à Dinant. Poète, comédien et metteur en scène, il travaille également dans les prisons de Marche-en-Famenne et d'Arlon en tant que conseiller laïque.

En 2019, il co-fonde l'Absolu Théâtre avec Charlotte Simon. C'est avec cette compagnie qu'il écrit et met en scène les spectacles *A-vide* et *J'aimerais mourir sous un orme*.

Animateur de nombreux ateliers d'écriture, il donne ponctuellement des modules d'écriture dramatique au Conservatoire royal de Bruxelles.

Charlotte Simon est née en 1997. Comédienne et danseuse, elle travaille en tant qu'interprète dans le projet *Espaces Vers* et co-dirige l'*Absolu Théâtre.* Elle se prête au jeu de l'illustration pour la première fois dans le cadre de l'écriture de ce recueil.

Bibliographie

Puisque l'aube est défaite, poèmes, M.E.O, 2013, prix Georges Lockem de l'Académie royale de langue et littérature françaises de Belgique

Io, la belle, poèmes, éditions Bleu d'encre, 2018

Du feu dans les brindilles, poèmes, éditions Bleu d'encre, 2019

Le cœur en Lesse, nouvelles, M.E.O, 2019

A-vide suivi de *J'aimerais mourir sous un orme*, théâtre, éditions Les oiseaux de nuit, 2021

Terre silence, à paraître aux éditions Bleu d'encre, prix Grand'Ry de l'Association des Écrivains Belges (AEB).

Collection dirigée par : Collana diretta da
Dante Bertoni

Titres déjà parus en Rootleg · Titoli già pubblicati in Rootleg

#1 Le droit à la parole / El derecho a la palabra Ada Mondès
#2 Christ et le Tigre / Cristo e la Tigre Davide Colasante
#3 Ensauvagement – Le petit livre de la colère Gioia Kayaga
#4 Une longue dissonance Tom Nisse

*que les livres circulent... la photocopie/le numérique
ne tuent que ce qui est déjà mort...*

retrouvez tous nos livres sur www.maelstromreevolution.org
et dans notre boutique **maelstrÖm 4 1 4**
364 chaussée de Wavre / BE-1040 Etterbeek

ISBN 978-2-87505-388-6
Dépôt légal — 2021 — D/2021/9407/5

Imprimé dans la dignité en Belgique sur les presses
de la Maison de la Poésie d'Amay